Please (

MW00441363

I want to keep in touch with you and send you inspirational emails occasionally.

I have 12 pages of Healing Scriptures I want to get into your hands. When you are sick, or know someone who is sick, read them out loud. The Word of God is medicine and has the power to heal your whole being. I would also like to send you free downloads, and I mean FREE.

https://www.spiritfilledcatholic.com/downloads

You can email me at if you need prayer or want to join any of my prayer groups.

mbwuenschel@gmail.com

You can also purchase my book "Your thoughts are Killing You" on my website.

https://www.spiritfilledcatholic.com/

Copyright © 2020 by
Spirit-Filled Catholic Publishing

All rights reserved. No part of this publication may be reproduced, distributed, or transmitted in any form or by any means, including photocopying, recording, or other electronic or mechanical methods, without the prior written permission of the publisher, except in the case of brief quotations embodied in reviews and certain other non-commercial uses permitted by copyright law.

All Scripture References are from the New American Bible Revised Edition (NABRE) unless otherwise noted.

New American Bible, revised edition Scripture texts in this work are taken from the *New American Bible, revised edition* © 2010, 1991, 1986, 1970 Confraternity of Christian Doctrine, Washington, D.C. and are used by permission of the copyright owner. All Rights Reserved. No part of the New American Bible may be reproduced in any form without permission in writing from the copyright owner.

New Living Translation (NLT) Some content taken from the Holy Bible, New Living Translation, copyright © 1996, 2004, 2015. Used by permission of Tyndale House Publishers, Inc., Carol Stream, Illinois 60188. All rights reserved.

ACTS IS A PRAYER format that works anywhere and anytime. It is easy to remember and helps you to stay focused on God during your prayer time.

God wants an intimate relationship with you. The more time you spend with Him, the closer to Him you will grow. The first and most important commandment is to love the Lord your God.

> **Matthew 22:36-38** *"Teacher, which commandment in the law is the greatest?" He said to him, "You shall love the Lord, your God, with all your heart, with all your soul, and with all your mind. This is the greatest and the first commandment.*

How do we love the Lord our God with all our heart if we don't spend time with Him? The Acts prayer format is a way to help you to know and love the Lord by spending quality time with Him and allowing Him to minister to you. It's time for us to grow up in our faith and to turn from relying solely on rote prayers. This takes practice and determination, not because it's hard, but because the devil does not want us to pray and will keep us from evolving if he can. The ACTS prayer is intended to help us grow by providing a helpful tool that will teach us how to pray spontaneously and keep us praying.

Jesus prayed. If He spent time with God in prayer, don't you think you need to also? The Bible says to pray fervently, and earnestly. Paul says to pray always *(1 Thessalonians 5:17)*.

> **Psalm 141:2** *Let my prayer be incense before you; my uplifted hands an evening offering.*

> **James 4:8** *Come near to God and He will come near to you.*

> **James 5:16** *The fervent prayer of a righteous person is very powerful.*

5

If God said it in His word, it is true. Imagine what God can accomplish in you and through you if you take the time to enter into His presence and spend time with Him.

God tells us to seek first the Kingdom of God, and everything will be given to us. All our needs will be met by seeking after Him. If you don't believe this, see Matthew 6:31-33 and hear it from God Himself. We follow Him, and He takes care of us. He says that He takes care of everything. Can it really be that good? Follow Him, and He does the rest.

Following God, knowing him and doing His will is not supposed to be burdensome. He doesn't hide from us and deliberately make the road bumpy. With or without Him the road will be bumpy, but how much better knowing the God of the Universe is your shield, your protection, your champion, defender, advocate, fortress, deliverer, and ever-present help in time of need.

This is God's promise to His children.

Spend time with Him and keep spending time with him. Don't just try it and give up when things don't immediately change. Hang in there. It didn't take you overnight to get where you are today and may not take you overnight to learn how to live the "good life." If you remain in him and in His word you will bear much fruit. Jesus says in John 15:7, *"If you remain in me and my words remain in you, ask for whatever you want and it will be done for you."* He will gladly reveal to you, His purpose and will for your life if you persevere. You will not only know what to do, but He will equip you to do it and will give you the hunger and desire to do what He has called you to do.

Following God is completely fulfilling and rewarding.

Follow the steps outlined in "ACTS." These steps will provide you with a guide to get you started, keep you on track and keep you going.

'ACTS' helps keep you focused on God. The devil will try to steal this time from you and keep you distracted. He hates God and doesn't want you growing in your relationship with God. He has no power over you, however he will exert his influence and do whatever it takes to distract and deceive you.

Before you begin your prayer time, grab your Bible and a notebook so you can write down what God is teaching you. You may at first record only the the Bible chapter and verse, but soon you will be jotting down something about the passage that appealed to you and eventually all that God is teaching you in His word. If you pursue God, you will find Him and when you do find God, He will make himself so appealing you can't stop seeking him. The more you seek, the more you find. You can't over seek Him; He is limitless. He is never-ending, and his goodness, joy and excitement is infinite.

He is the answer we are all searching for. The gift that keeps on giving.

INCORPORATE THE WORD of God into your prayer time. The Psalms are full of words of praise (See appendix for a list of praise statements that were inspired by the Word of God). Most of the Bible can be prayed. You will discover that almost everything you read can be turned into a prayer. The book of Colossians, for example, is one long prayer. See examples below.

Here are examples of how to read and then pray God's Word.

> **Psalm 27 says...** *"Though an army besiege me, though war break out against me I will remain confident in you, oh Lord."*

"Lord I believe you and trust you. I am confident you are coming through for me no matter what it looks like around me."

Colossians 1 says... *We continually ask God to fill you with the knowledge of His will through all the wisdom and understanding that the Spirit gives, so that you may live a life worthy of the Lord and please Him in every way: bearing fruit in every good work, growing in the knowledge of God.*

Pray that for someone or for yourself.

"Lord I ask you to fill me with the knowledge of your will, fill me with wisdom and understanding. I want to live a life worthy of you Lord. I want to please you in every way and grow in the knowledge of you."

Psalm 20 says... *"Some trust in chariots and some in horses, but we trust in the name of the Lord our God. They are brought to their knees and fall, but we rise up and stand firm.*

I trust in you Lord. I will not doubt your love for me. Some trust in their fortunes and positions, but I trust you will provide for me.

THE WORD OF GOD is a powerful way to pray. The Bible is God's word, and when we read and study it for ourselves, we begin to know God's word and believe His word to be true. We begin to believe that God is true to His word and that we can bank on it. We will start to pray powerful prayers of faith. Jesus said in Mark 11 *"Therefore I tell you, whatever you ask for in prayer, believe that you have received it, and it will be yours."*

INVITE THE HOLY SPIRIT every time you open the Bible to read, pray or study. Jesus said "I have much more to tell you, but you cannot bear it now. But when he comes, the Spirit of truth, he will guide you to all truth" (John 16:12-13). I try never to read the Bible without the presence of the Holy Spirit. I endeavor to remember to invite Him every time.

PRAY - Holy Spirit, You are the giver of life. Bring life to my prayer time and Bible reading time. Lead me to the truth and open up the Word of God so I may understand. Make the Bible come to life.

READY TO BEGIN?

PAUSE TO HEAR FROM THE LORD between each section. Do not pause too long. You don't want your mind to wander. Just pause long enough to hear from God. You may not hear from God in the beginning but persevere and you will. More than likely you will hear from God later in the day, perhaps during work, chores or through someone else or a circumstance.

Let God know you are serious about Him. Take time to pray daily. Whether you hear immediately from Him or not, you will hear from Him if you persevere.

"This is the confidence we have in approaching God: that if we ask anything according to his will, he hears us." 1 John 5:14

A - Adoration
(Praise and Worship)

PRAISE:
To express approval or admiration of. Commend; extol; offer homage.

ADORATION:
Deep love and respect. Worship; veneration:

Always begin prayer with Praise and Adoration. Always! The Israelites began their prayer time with Praise and Adoration and so does the Church. Enter into your time with God, no matter how long or short, with praise and worship. I always begin with a song, a psalm or I read from the praise statements. (See Appendix) The Bible says in Psalm 100:4 that we are to "enter His courts with praise." We are to enter into His presence with praise.

Tell God how much you love Him. Tell God how awesome and wonderful He is. I have found many people to struggle with this at first, but only at first. We are tempted to go right to petitioning God so make it a point to praise God for a while; be deliberate about it. Make a decision to first praise God who is worthy of praise and eventually it will become second nature.

When the Jairus, a synagogue official, saw Jesus, he fell at his feet. Jairus' daughter was dying and he begged Jesus to come and lay hands on her. Before he asked Jesus, however, he worshipped him. Matthew's version shows Jairus kneeling before him acknowledging him openly as Lord and God.   When the Canaanite woman in Matthew 15 approached Jesus she too fell at His feet in worship as she pleaded for the Lord's help.

Psalm 145 tells us to praise God using our voice. Don't just think about how great God is, say it. Verbalize it. Let God hear you. Let the devil hear you.

Psalm 145	Definitions
I will **extol** you, my God and King; I will **bless** your name forever and ever. Every day I will **bless** you; I will **praise** your name forever and ever. Great is the Lord and worthy of much praise, whose grandeur is beyond understanding. One generation **praises** your deeds to the next and **proclaims** your mighty works. They **speak** of the splendor of your majestic glory, **tell** of your wonderful deeds. They **speak** of the power of your awesome acts and **recount** your great deeds.	**Extol -** praise highly **Bless** - speak well of **Praise** - expression of approval (it must be expressed not just thought) **Proclaim** - declare publicly **Speak -** utter words **Tell -** say, make known, express in words **Recount** - narrate, relate in detail.

Praising God is telling Him who He is and how great He is. We praise Him because He is God and because of the wonderful things He does. As we praise Him for who He is, we see Him in His true light and character. We begin to see Him as the almighty God of the universe. Not only is God put in proper perspective but so are we and so are all of our circumstances and troubles. As God is magnified, our troubles become small in comparison.

There is power in our words. There is power in the words of praise coming out of our mouths to change us, to change our minds, and shut the enemy down (see more on this later). So let your words declare the greatness and glory of God. There is power in them! More power than you know!

Psalm 66:2-4 *"Shout joyfully to God, all the earth; sing of His glorious name; give Him glorious praise. Say to God: "How awesome your deeds! Before your great strength, your enemies cringe. All the earth falls in worship before you; they sing of you, sing of your name!"*

If we begin with praise and do nothing else, we have prayed a perfect and complete prayer. If it is all we do, all we get around to, it is enough; more than enough.

When Jesus taught us how to pray, I don't think He meant to give us a memorized prayer, necessarily. He taught us how to approach His Father in order to have a relationship with Him. He wants us in

Psalm 95:1-3
Come, let us sing for joy to the LORD; let us shout aloud to the Rock of our salvation. Let us come before Him with thanksgiving and extol Him with music and song. For the LORD is the great God, the great King above all gods.

Psalm 145:1-3
I will extol you, my God and king; I will bless your name forever and ever. Every day I will bless you; I will praise your name forever and ever. Great is the Lord and worthy of much praise, whose grandeur is beyond understanding.

Psalm 149:1-3
Sing to the Lord a new song, his praise in the assembly of the faithful. Let Israel be glad in its Maker, the people of Zion rejoice in their king. Let them praise his name in dance, make music with tambourine and lyre.

> **Psalm 47:2-3** Oh, clap your hands, all you peoples! Shout to God with the voice of triumph! For the Lord Most High is awesome; He is a great King over all the earth.
>
> **Psalm 33:1-3** Rejoice, you righteous, in the LORD; praise from the upright is fitting. Give thanks to the LORD on the harp; on the ten stringed lyre offer praise. Sing to Him a new song; skillfully play with a joyful chant.
>
> **Psalm 34:1-4** I will bless the LORD at all times; His praise shall always be in my mouth. My soul will glory in the LORD;   let the poor hear and be glad. Magnify the LORD with me, and   let us exalt His name together.

conversation with God. Let's look at the "Our Father" found in Scripture.

In thiHe teaches us first and foremost to praise God. "Hallowed be thy name" (holy are you, Lord; holy is your name). He wants us to recognize God's greatness, and by speaking it, we may believe it and remember it. When we praise God, we give Him His due. We show Him how much we admire Him, believe in Him and trust Him. When we praise Him, we are honoring and worshiping Him. We let Him know that He truly is our God. We let Him know He is worthy of praise when we praise Him by opening our mouths and speaking. We let others around us know who our God is when we proclaim His goodness and glory to others.

Praising God may not come naturally. You may have to force it at first. When you do, it will begin to come more readily. Praising the football team when they score a touchdown, comes naturally, but when you praise God, it feels awkward. Do it anyway! Do it awkward; you will touch God's heart. He is so pleased when you praise Him even though you don't yet understand why. Do it just because you want to do something just for Him.

Why praise God? In the Bible, God commands us to praise Him. He knows we need it. It is so important to Him; He commands us over and over again in the Psalms.

Why does God want our praises? Why does He command us to give Him honor and adoration? God doesn't need our praises, but He knows we need to do it. When we praise God, we turn our hearts and our minds to Him. We look at Him, dwell on Him, we turn our attention to our God. When we speak words of praise about God to others or in prayer, our mind and thoughts follow. God deserves our full attention. Our minds like to wander, but as we praise Him and search for words to describe Him and honor Him, our thoughts are taken captive. When our attention has turned to God, and we recognize how big and good and powerful He is, all of a sudden our problems seem so small.

God wants us to praise Him and declare His greatness, so we know who to run to, who to go to for answers and help. God says in His word that He is "our ever present help in time of need." He wants us to know this so we run to Him in our hour of need. He doesn't say that just so He can turn His back and say no. He says it because He means it. He wants us to know who He is. The Bible declares how awesome the Lord is, how mighty and glorious are His deeds not to boast about Himself so that you will know what He will do for you. There is nothing God won't do for you.

Psalm 145:11-12 *They tell of the glory of your kingdom and speak of your might, so that all people may know of your mighty acts and the glorious splendor of your kingdom.*

DEVIL FLEES WHEN WE PRAISE

Praise is a powerful weapon against the enemy. Do you feel anger, worry, stress, hatred, or criticism welling up in you? Begin to praise God. The devil hates it when you praise God. He will do anything and everything to get you stop or better yet never to begin at all. You will see the worry, fear, etc. leave, run when you voice your praise. Read how Joshua defeated Jericho with a trumpet blast and a shout of praise in Joshua 6 or how Jehoshaphat defeated three armies attacking his country with PRAISE in 2 Chronicles 20.

Praise, worship, and adoration are not something we do only when it feels right, or we feel like it. Sometimes it is a sacrifice. I don't think the army felt like walking around Jericho singing and praising God and blowing the trumpet. THEY DID IT BECAUSE GOD SAID TO. We OFFER it up to God because He is our God. The Bible says to offer your bodies as living sacrifices. It's a discipline. Praise Him whether you feel like it or not. Don't go with your feelings they can be misleading. God honors your praises especially when they are given during times when you would rather not.

Psalm 50:14 Offer praise as your sacrifice to God; fulfill your vows to the Most High. Verse 23 - Those who offer praise as a sacrifice honor me.

Hebrews 13:15 Through Jesus, therefore, let us continually offer to God a sacrifice of praise, the fruit of lips that openly profess His name.

Romans 12:1 Therefore, I urge you, brothers and sisters, in view of God's mercy, to offer your bodies as a living sacrifice, holy and pleasing to God—this is your true and proper worship.

Don't quit, embrace praise and enter into it. Don't rush through it. We prefer to pray for others or say our rote prayers. Praising God requires discipline. Remember, if all we do is praise God we have done enough praying, so this is worth the effort.

So how do we praise, worship and adore God in prayer? We praise God with our voices primarily as we sing and shout, but also with instruments, and with our bodies. Clapping, dancing, raising our hands, kneeling and falling prostrate before the Lord, are all works of praise and worship. ENJOY the Lord, laugh and sing with Him. Celebrate Him. Remember the woman with the alabaster jar of very expensive perfume? She opened it and poured it on Jesus' feet in Mark 14. We can never over do worship. We can never give too much to God. It may be embarrassing to others, but God will accept your praise and worship. When David danced before the Lord, he was criticized by his wife. He said

> **2 Samuel 6:21-22** *"It was before the Lord, who chose me rather than your father or anyone from his house when he appointed me ruler over the Lord's people Israel—I will celebrate before the Lord. 22 I will become even more undignified than this, and I will be humiliated in my own eyes.*

> **2 Samuel 6: 14-15** *Then David danced before the Lord with all his might, and David was wearing a linen ephod. So David and all the house of Israel brought up the ark of the Lord with shouting and with the sound of the trumpet.*

Words of praise do not come naturally; we need to practice. One great way to begin is to open the Bible to the Psalms. The Psalms are filled with praise especially the first few verses. Here are a few to get you started.

Psalm 18:1-3
I love you, Lord, my strength. The Lord is my rock, my
fortress and my deliverer; my God is my rock, in whom
I take refuge, my shield and the horn of my salvation, my
stronghold. I called to the Lord, who is worthy of praise,
and I have been saved from my enemies.

Psalm 150: 1-6   Hallelujah!   Praise God in His holy
sanctuary; give praise in the mighty dome of heaven. Give
praise for His mighty deeds, praise Him for His great
majesty. Give praise with blasts upon the horn, praise
Him with harp and lyre. Give praise with tambourines and
dance, praise Him with strings and pipes. Give praise with
crashing cymbals, praise Him with sounding cymbals. Let
everything that has breath give praise to the LORD!
Hallelujah!

Psalm 100:1-5   Shout joyfully to the LORD, all you lands;
serve the LORD with gladness; Come before Him with
joyful song. Know that the LORD is God, he made us, we
belong to Him, we are His people, the flock He shepherds.
Enter His gates with thanksgiving, His courts with praise.
Give thanks to Him, bless His name; good indeed is the
LORD, His mercy endures forever, His faithfulness lasts
through every generation.

Now try it, begin your sentences with "YOU ARE" and follow up with words that describe God.

A - Adoration - (Praise and Worship)

YOU ARE... The creator of the universe, the everlasting God.

You are my Father in Heaven, the ever-loving and ever-living God who can do all things and cares about us His children.

You are my rock, my fortress, my God in whom I trust.

You are my refuge, my safe place, my shield, and protection.

You are my father and my provider.

You are holy, righteous and true.

You are the author of life, in You we live, and move and have our being.

You are glorious, wonderful, forever and ever.

You are compassionate, faithful, and loving toward all you have made.

You are the prince of peace, the great I Am.

You are all powerful, almighty God of heaven and earth.

You move Mountains for us Lord,

You move heaven and earth for us your children.

You are the way, the truth, and the life.

You are my ever present help in time of need.

You are the King of Kings, the Lord of all Lords.

You are the alpha, the omega, the first and the last.

Jesus, you are my Lord and Savior.

You are worthy of all my praise, love, time and devotion.

You are...

When you run out of words, start praising Him in tongues, worship Him by lifting up your arms to God, go down on your knees, get on your face before Him.

See how the Israelites worshiped God in 1 Chronicles 29.

1 Chronicles 29:20-22

Then David told the whole assembly, "Now bless the LORD your God!" And the whole assembly blessed the LORD, the God of their ancestors, bowing down in homage before the LORD and before the king. On the following day they brought sacrifices and burnt offerings to the LORD, a thousand bulls, a thousand rams, and a thousand lambs, together with their libations and many other sacrifices for all Israel; and on that day, they ate and drank in the LORD's presence with great rejoicing.

For help with praise see appendix (Praise statements and the Litany of Praise)

C- Confession

There are two parts to confession, and both are important and life changing.

Part One - Confess your sins to God, priest or one another.
Part Two - Confess who you are in Christ, what is yours, what you believe, and who you believe in.

READY TO GROW UP IN THE HOLY SPIRIT. Call on the Holy Spirit. He is our helper.

Part One

CONFESS
TO DECLARE OR AC-
KNOWLEDGE ONE'S SINS.

Allow the Holy Spirit to guide you to confess your sins.
DO NOT look for your sins or spend time trying to figure them out or remember them. Let the Holy Spirit show you. Ask Him. Say "Holy Spirit show me where I have failed you, or sinned against God. He will show you, and when He does, ask for forgiveness and move on. The Bible says in **1 John 1:9** *"If we confess our sins, He is faithful and just and will forgive us our sins and purify us from all unrighteousness."*

So ask and be done with it. Do not dwell or remain in guilt and shame. Rise up and walk. The devil wants you on the sidelines, out of his way. He wants you to remain guilty, accused and depressed, so you will be ineffective for God's Kingdom. When you remain guilty and shameful, you are rejecting Jesus' forgiveness. Simple as that. You are rejecting Jesus' finished work on the cross.

NOW SAY With Confidence "I am forgiven." Jesus didn't die so you would stay unforgiven. He died to forgive you. Now act like you are forgiven and get over it. He paid a high price for your freedom. I don't think He wants to see you still in prison and feeling guilty. So let him take your sins. Don't let his death be in vain.

Part Two

CONFESS
TO PROFESS YOUR FAITH.
To DECLARE THE TRUTH;
WHAT YOU BELIEVE IN.
To SAY, to SPEAK; acknowledge, admit or own.

Make a confession of faith to God. WHAT? This is so new to us but life-changing. You will grow in Him beyond your wildest imaginations when you change the way you think and speak. Where in the "A - adoration" we began our sentences with "You are".... Here we begin with "I am" or "I."

Before we can love, honor and serve God with all our hearts as He expects us to and commands us to, we have to begin at least with saying it. Say it out loud. Hear yourself say those words.

"Jesus, I love you with all my heart, soul, mind and strength."

You may not feel like you love Him or know for sure you love Him. Say it anyway. It is the beginning. The feelings will follow. The first time you say "Jesus I love you," it will seem so foreign and awkward. Are you willing to feel foolish and awkward for God? Are you willing to say I love you to your Father in heaven who loves you so much He sent His son to die just for you?

If you have doubt about your relationship with Jesus, then this may be a good time to surrender to Him if you have never done so...

Prayer of Surrender

Today I surrender to You Lord Jesus. I surrender to You because I trust You. I surrender all to You, my health, my family, my finances, my work, my relationships, my successes and failures. I release it all to You.
I surrender to You Lord my fears, my insecurities, the past, the present, and the future. I belong to You.

Now it's time to make some confessions. How do we do this and what does it mean? Making a confession is simply speaking out loud the truth about who you are, what is yours and who you belong to. Let yourself hear these words you are saying.

The following **"I AM's"** are taken from verses found in the Bible. This is what God says about you and me. So it has to be true. It is His desire for us to know who He is and what He thinks about us. The Bible says that all of God's promises and blessings are ours because we are in Christ Jesus. God made lots of promises to us, to heal, protect and care for us. There are also curses in the Bible for those who reject God and follow after other gods. Jesus took all the curses so we could have all the blessings. Are you in Christ Jesus? If you are, then all of God's promises are for you.

If God says they are yours and for you, then it's time for you to own them. It's time for you to start saying what God says about you and not what the devil says about you. Just because you think something is true doesn't mean it is true. Just because you believe something to be true about you doesn't mean it is. You may have been told your whole life that you are lazy and good for nothing. You can keep believing that about yourself or make a decision to change your thoughts. If you keep saying I am so tired, lazy, bummed, depressed, an idiot, forgetful, or sick, you will remain that way.

What you say is important. Words are powerful. We are lifted up by just a word. We are brought down by just a word. God created the world with just a word. Jesus healed the sick with just a word, and He gave us the same power. We can build ourselves up or tear ourselves down with a word. We can make or break someone's day by our words. Our words are more than just suggestive; they have supernatural power.

Jesus said in Mark 11:22-23 *Jesus said to them in reply, "Have faith in God. Amen, I say to you, whoever says to this mountain, 'Be lifted up and thrown into the sea,' and does not doubt in his heart but believes that what he says will happen, it shall be done for him. Therefore I tell you, all that you ask for in prayer, believe that you will receive it and it shall be yours.*

Start saying supernatural things. Put your words to work and change your circumstances. You may be sick, but if God says you are healed, start "SAYING" "I am healed." You can say "I am so sick, " but that will not help you get better. If you prayed to God for healing, then start acting like you believe he heard you and healed you! Read what I just said a few more times till it sinks in. You may be saying how do I know God wants me healed? How do I know that God says I am healed? (Read Matthew 8:16-17, or Psalm 103:3, or Isaiah 53:5, Mark 1:40-42)

God thinks more highly of you than you do. Let's change our opinion or perception about ourselves by changing the way we speak to ourselves or think about ourselves. It's hard to change our thoughts, but one effective way is to change what we say. Our mind and thoughts will follow. You can't keep thinking you are weak when you keep saying you are strong. Change your words starting today.

LET's declare (so all will know, even the devil and all his demons) that .....

Jesus died for me. Jesus loves me. God sent His son for me. Jesus sits at the right hand of the father forever interceding for me. Jesus became sin so I could become righteous. I am the righteousness of God in Christ Jesus. He died for all my sins, even the ones I am going to commit in the future, what an awesome God He is. I am blessed because my sins are not only forgiven but God Himself chose to forget them.

The Lord protects me from all my enemies. I am protected. No harm or disease, pestilence or disaster will come near me. My enemies will come at me from one direction but flee from me in seven. I am blessed by the Lord, and so is my family.

My finances are blessed because I am His, and He is my provider. I do not worry about anything. I trust Him and will not fear or worry about my life or my finances. He has taken care of everything.

Thoughts follow our words; faith follows our words:
So let's speak in faith though we may not yet believe it or see it.
Let's say it anyway.

I AM (I)...

I am forgiven, My past has been washed away, and I am brand new because I am yours, and you make me new.

I surrender myself to you, Lord. I believe you love me and care about me. I trust you; I trust you with my health, my life, my children, my future.

I am your child. I am accepted and adopted into the family of God. I am a daughter of the most High God.

I am strong in the Lord and in His mighty power because He makes me strong. He is my strength.

The Holy Spirit lives in me.

Greater is He that is in me than He that is in the world.

I am free from blemish, cleansed, holy and blameless in your sight because I am in Christ. I have been saved from God's wrath because I am in Christ, hidden in Him.

Because Jesus took my sins and my sicknesses and diseases with Him on the cross, I am delivered from every evil.

I have been redeemed. I am His chosen possession.

I trust you, Lord. You say you will never leave me, and I believe you.

I am convinced you love me and are protecting me and keeping me safe. I am victorious. I am an overcomer;

I am His child, His heir. I can do all things through you Jesus, who strengthens me.

I can bend a bow of bronze; I can scale a wall.

You are my shield, my hiding place, my strong tower.

1 Corinthians 6:11, 2 Corinthians 5:17, Psalm 51:2, 1 Peter 5:7, Psalm 37:7-9, Proverbs 3:5, Ephesians 1:5, Ephesians 6:10, 1 John 4:4, Colossians 1:22, Colossians 3:3, Ephesians 1:7, Hebrews 13:5, 1 Corinthians 15:57, Romans 8:37, Romans 8:17, Galatians 4:7, Philippians 4:13, Psalm 18:29, Psalm 119:114

I am a good provider.
I am a good wife, mother.
I am a good Father, husband.
I am healthy. I am trustworthy. I am bold.
I am confident. I walk by faith, not by sight.
I am well; I am healed.
My God supplies all of my needs.

I am kind; I am joyful.
I have the joy of the Lord as my strength.
I am filled with peace and stay in peace.
I am self-controlled, gentle.
I am patient; I live in the Spirit, and my mind is on spiritual things.
I am not conceited, easily angered, envious or easily offended.
I do not throw fits of rage; I am calm, full of wisdom and
understanding.
I am thoughtful, considerate and compassionate.
I am not jealous or envious of others; I am not self-centered or
rude.
I am meek and humble not proud and boastful.
I do not spend time thinking evil thoughts.
I keep no record of others' faults and failings.
I do not delight in evil. I am faithful and true.
I am trustworthy and honest. You can count on me.
I will love you, Lord, forever.
I can move mountains. I will not be shaken. I will not shrink back
in the face of persecution. I will not fear though the earth give way,
and the mountains fall into the sea, though the waters roar and
foam and the mountains quake. Even then I am confident because
my confidence comes from you.

ARE YOU SICK
SAY THIS OUT LOUD - DECLARE IT

These are mostly scripture and since scripture is a weapon let's wield it. The Bible says the sword of the Spirit is the word of God. Faith comes by hearing not from having heard that is why it is important to hear the word every day, declare it, and read it.   It is important because we need to know and be confident in God and what He says. MORE CONFIDENT in Him and His promises to us than we are in what the doctors or the report or the symptoms say.

"I declare I am well because Jesus said 'ask me anything in my name and I will do it so that the Son may bring glory to the Father, ask me anything in my name and I will do it.' Because of HIM, I can boldly declare I am well because I believe Him and know He is faithful to His word. I receive your love and healing dear God and thank you for healing me. Sickness and disease, I declare to you that my God is greater, my God is stronger, my God is higher than you and anything you can throw at me. **John 14:13-14**

I declare Lord Jesus; You took my sins, sickness, and disease with you to the cross where it was nailed for evermore. I accept this gift and believe you did it for me. I choose to walk by faith, not by sight. I believe you are healing me, and I do not believe the symptoms or what I feel. I believe you more and your word which says You took our infirmities with you to the cross, and you bore our diseases. **Matt 8:16-17**

I declare I am ransomed, delivered and rescued from all my fears. I declare that I called, and you heard me. You are my God in whom I trust. No weapon formed against me will prosper because you are watching over me. When I drink deadly poison, medicine or chemo, I will not be harmed. I am a believer. Jesus is Lord of my life. God said He will sustain me on my sickbed and restore me to health, and I believe Him. The Lord defends me and protects me from all disease, plagues, and pestilence. He promises, and I believe. **Psalm 34:4-6, Isaiah 54:17, Mark 16:18, Psalm 41:3, Psalm 91:5-6**

I declare today - I trust Jesus has my back. The spirit of infirmity has no hold on me. I declare my faith in Jesus who promises to take care of me, my family and my future generations. Sickness and disease stop here. It will not be passed down to future generations. **Luke 13:12**

I declare I am free from the curse and so is my family. I will run and not grow weary; I will walk and not grow faint, though a thousand fall at my side it will not come near me. God has plans for my future." **Galatians 3:13, Isaiah 40, Psalm 91:7, Jeremiah 29:11**

"Is 40: Even youths grow tired and weary, and young men stumble and fall; but those who hope in the Lord will renew their strength. They will soar on wings like eagles; they will run and not grow weary, they will walk and not be faint."

T - Thanking God

It is always appropriate to thank God. Everything is from Him. The Bible says all good gifts come from Him. So thank Him and try to thank Him for something new every time you pray.

When we thank God, we are humbling ourselves and acknowledging that He is the one who should get the credit. We are giving God glory. We are admitting that everything is a gift and not something that we earned based on our own works or goodness. Thanking God is acknowledging His hand in the good things you do or receive.

Thanking God lets Him know you believe in Him and need Him. We like to think we deserve certain things because of our own worthiness or effort or based on our success and accomplishments. Jesus says without him we are nothing and can do nothing (John 15:5-6).
"I bought this house; it is mine, I saved up for it; I worked for it."
"I am a doctor, lawyer."

When we thank God we are giving Him all the credit.

> **Ephesians 5:19-20** *Instead, be filled with the Spirit, speaking to one another with psalms, hymns, and songs from the Spirit. Sing and make music from your heart to the Lord, always giving thanks to God the Father for everything, in the name of our Lord Jesus Christ.*

Thank God for what you are praying for. Thank Him even if you don't see the answer yet. Thank Him ahead of time. It is a sign of faith letting God know you believe Him, you trust Him with the prayer. It lets Him know you have faith in Him for the answer.

Mark 11:24 *Therefore I tell you, whatever you ask for in prayer, believe that you have received it, and it will be yours.*

God tells us in His word to thank Him, not because he needs thanks but because it's good for us. Psalm 118 says to "Give thanks to the Lord for He is good."

Thank you Lord.....

I thank you, Lord, that whatever I put my hand to will prosper. Thank you for my health. Thank you for watching out for me, for never leaving me. Thank you, Father, for loving me and for sending your son to me. Thank you for eyes that work, thank you for my arms and legs, for my talents. Thank you for the special people you have put in my life.

S- Supplication (Intercession)

```
Supplication:
humble prayer,
entreaty, or petition
```

This is your opportunity to ask. Go ahead, ask. God wants us to ask. He says "And whatever you ask in my name, I will do, so that the Father may be glorified in the Son" (John 14:14). He goes on to say it again. "If you ask anything of me in my name, I will do it." He doesn't add any buts with it. We like to, though, but not Jesus. He says "ask me anything," and he means it. It is as if he is saying "watch me show off how great my father is." ASK. Jesus gave us His name, and He wants us to go the Father and tell Him "Jesus sent me. He told me I could come to you and ask anything, and you would do it." Be bold.

Ask big - God will not be glorified if we only ask for the common place or ordinary stuff. Go for it, ask crazy. Now and then we need to ask GOD SIZED prayers and increase our faith. Our faith and trust in God will grow as we ask Him and watch Him answer. You know it's God when you ask for something only God can do.

When we ask, we then have the opportunity to receive, and a reason to praise Him all over again and tell everyone about Him. We have a testimony, a witness of God's power, and love for us.

He wants us to ask because He loves us. God loves us and wants to come through for us for our sake. He is our "ever present help in time of need," the Bible says. He wouldn't tell us that if it wasn't true. He is not trying to trick us. Trust in Him.

Matthew 7:9-12   *"Which of you, if your son asks for bread, will give him a stone? Or if he asks for a fish, will give him a snake? If you, then, though you are evil, know how to give good gifts to your children, how much more will your Father in heaven give good gifts to those who ask Him! So in everything, do to others what you would have them do to you, for this sums up the Law and the Prophets.*

When we ask we are showing God, we need Him. We admit we are powerless over the situation or circumstance without him. It allows God to be God and expresses our need for a savior. When you ask God and let others know you are asking. Be willing to go out on a limb, to trust God to come through for you in front of others. Be willing to be ridiculed. We have hope, and our hope is in our Lord.

Ask for your family, friends, fellow workers, church, church leaders, community leaders, government, schools, teachers, children's friends and anyone the Holy Spirit brings to mind.

Ask for yourself, ask to grow in age, grace, and wisdom. Ask to be filled with the Holy Spirit. You will soon bear much fruit for the Kingdom. Ask for the gifts of the Holy Spirit. Desire to be a fruitful and productive member of the kingdom. We can only do that filled with the Holy Spirit. Ask the Holy Spirit to give you a hunger for Him and His Word. Ask him to give you faith to move mountains.

When interceding for others or for a situation that causes you grief or stress of some kind, pray till you have peace. Don't be afraid to press in. Don't be quick to say well it's all in God's timing, or it must be His will. God may, in fact, be waiting on you. The best advice I ever received was to pray till I received peace.

God made a way for us to come right into the throne room of God. Jesus died for us so we can come boldly and confidently to God through Him. Don't worry if you don't deserve it. None of us deserve anything. That is why Jesus came. He is the only one worthy to enter the throne room. None of us have access in our state of sin. So, God, Himself made a way for us, and that way was His son. Jesus died so we could come to the Father through Him. We come in His name not our own. Jesus is sitting at the right hand of the father ever interceding for us. What are you waiting for? He did it for you. He loves you. If you were the only person left on earth, God would have sent His son to die for you.

SAY THIS PRAYER FOR HEALING

You may not believe it at first, but the more you say it, the more you will believe it.

"I believe that I am well, I may not feel well, but I walk by faith, not by sight, faith that Jesus took my sickness and disease with him on the cross. I am strong in the Lord, and because His mighty power is in me. The greater one lives in me, and my body, muscles, nerves, tissue, organs, and all my systems are healed and whole and in good working order because I have faith in the name of Jesus. My body is healed, and well, and pain is leaving me because it must obey the word of God and because I come against it in the name of Jesus."

Just like the police officer can command you because he does so in the name of the law and the government that supports him, so can we come against evil in the name of Jesus.

The Bible says that God "gives strength to the fainting and he makes vigor abound for the weak and though young men grow faint and weary not so those who trust in the Lord. Those who hope in the Lord will renew their strength and will rise up on wings like the eagle's" Isaiah 40. I am your precious child, and my hope is in you, Lord. I trust you, and I believe my strength is being renewed, and I will run and not grow weary."

PRAYERS FOR HEALING CANCER

Today is the first day of the rest of your life; you are waking up refreshed in the blood of the lamb who cleansed you and made you white as snow and perfect and healed. None of the diseases of the Egyptians are on us his children (Deuteronomy 7:15).

The blessing of God is yours today and forever because you belong to Christ, and healing is your gift from God, and it is irrevocable (Romans 11:29). Jesus died and was buried and by the same Spirit that lives in us, He was raised from the dead and now because of his great love for us sits at the right hand of power forever interceding for us. Jesus is our Lord and Savior, and we are his great reward.

Declare it out loud today *"I am Jesus' reward and He is watching over me and protecting me.*
I am perfectly and wonderfully made. Jesus has healed me. By his stripes, I am healed. I will not fear, but I am standing my ground, and I WILL see the victory the Lord has won for me. Jesus is sitting at the right hand of God interceding on my behalf I will live and not die and declare the works of the Lord to the generations that follow me. I am more than a conqueror through Christ who strengthens me. The Lord has won this battle, and he has fought this enemy and won it just for me. Cancer is under feet. I am the head and not the tail. The word of God says that the Lord will beat down before me any enemy that rises up against me. They will come at me in one direction but will flee in seven directions. Devil, you come against me with fear and threats and intimidation, but I come against you in the name of Jesus. I am whole, and my body is healthy. Jesus is Lord of my body. Cancer, tumors, lesions and any and all corrupt cells in my body must leave in the name of Jesus. I command my body to rise up today and live pain-free and declare the works of the Lord.

Praise to the one who sits on the throne, all glory honor and praise to the king of kings."

PRAYER FOR HEALING of OTHERS

I believe in you Lord Jesus, help me with my unbelief. Holy Spirit I ask for the gift of faith to believe for this person who needs healing. You have the power to raise the dead and you live in me and you say that I too, will do what you do and even greater things! I come not in my own name nor in my own power or piety, but in the name of Jesus. You said I could ask for anything and I am asking for something you want more than I do. You want this for _____(name)_____ and have already provided the way. Jesus carried all our diseases and bore our pain and burdens and sickness (Matthew 8:16-17.) Every time Jesus tells us to ask the Father in his name, He follows it up with a promise that we will receive whatever we ask for.

Father may you be glorified through _____(name)_____. We believe Lord, and we walk by faith not by sight (2 Cor 5:17), faith in you and in your word which says "All that you ask for in prayer, believe that you will receive it and it shall be yours (Mark 11:22-25)." What a promise! We ask you to heal _____ and deliver her/him from ___(sickness)_____. We believe more in you Lord than in what it looks like, sounds like or feels like. We are standing on your word "He took away our infirmities and bore our diseases" (Matthew 8:17). We thank you ahead of time for _____'s healing from _____ . We come to you boldly and confidently because we come, not in our own name or in our own goodness, but in Jesus' name. Amen

God cannot resist us when we come in Jesus' name. He will do anything for Jesus. That is why Jesus gave us His name and told us to use it. We come in prayer believing we are good enough to ask because when we come in Jesus' name we are telling God, we believe Jesus has forgiven us all our sins and made us worthy to ask. We believe God is hearing our prayer and moving on _____'s behalf. Hebrews 4:16 says we can come boldly and confidently to the throne of grace. We come boldly to the throne of grace and mercy on behalf of _____ because God decided a long time ago that _____ was worth dying for. God sent His son to die for _____ and take his/her sins and sickness.

Mark 11:22-25

Jesus said to them in reply, **"Have faith in God.** Amen, I say to you, whoever says to this mountain, 'Be lifted up and thrown into the sea,' and does not doubt in his heart but believes that what he says will happen, it shall be done for him. Therefore I tell you, **all that you ask for in prayer, believe that you will receive it and it shall be yours.** When you stand to pray, forgive anyone against whom you have a grievance, so that your heavenly Father may in turn forgive you your transgressions."

Matthew 8:16-17

 When it was evening, they brought him many who were possessed by demons, and he drove out the spirits by a word and cured all the sick, 17 to fulfill what had been said by Isaiah the prophet: "He took away our infirmities and bore our diseases."

John 14:12-14

Very truly I tell you, whoever believes in me will do the works I have been doing, and they will do even greater things than these, because I am going to the Father. And I will do whatever you ask in my name, so that the Father may be glorified in the Son. You may ask me for anything in my name, and I will do it.

APPENDIX

PRAISE Statements / Scriptures

Why? because He is worth it. Because He tells us to over and over again in the scripture.

SAY THESE OUT LOUD as a way to express your praise to GodYou may respond to each phrase with *"Praise you Jesus"* or *"Thank you Lord"*.

You are the everlasting God, the creator of all things. The creator of the universe.

You are the ever-loving and ever-living God.

You are our hope, we trust You in everything and always.

You never let me down, I can count on you.

You never fail me. You are my Father who loves me.

You are dependable. I depend on you Lord Jesus

You are faithful and true to your Word. My future is in your hands, you promise me a future full of hope.

You promise that your children will not have to beg for bread so I trust you for my daily bread, both now and forever. I will not fear.

You never give up on me you never grow tired or weary.

You are our provider, you supply all our needs.

You open wide your hand and satisfy the desire of every living thing

You pardon all our sins and heal all our diseases.

You are the King of Kings, and Lord of all Lords. The great King over all God's. The Great I am.

You Lord are king. The world will surely stand fast, never to be shaken.

You are all powerful, nothing is too difficult for you.

With you ALL THINGS are possible.

Everything is possible for Him who believes.

You are our ever-present help in time of need.

You are near to all who call upon you in truth.

Justice and righteousness are the foundation of your throne.

Lord You are compassionate and gracious, slow to anger, abounding in love.

Your unfailing love is higher than the heavens. Your faithfulness reaches to the clouds.

You will never leave us nor forsake us.

You LORD take delight in me; You crown the humble with victory.

You are our defender. Our Strong Tower, our mighty fortress. **No weapon** formed against us can stand.

We are more than conquerors through You Lord Jesus.

If God is for us who can be against us.

You are FOR ME. I will not fear.

You redeem my life from the pit and crown me with love and compassion.

You satisfy my desires with good things so that my youth is renewed like the eagle's.

You move mountains for us, Lord,

You move heaven and earth for us, your children.

You do not treat us as our sins deserve or repay us according to our iniquities. For as high as the heavens are above the earth, so great is Your love for those of us who fear You; as far as the east is from the west, You have removed our transgressions from me. We are your children, heirs in your kingdom.

You are our great warrior. We never fight our battles alone.

You are our armor, our shield, our great protection.

You are the author of life, in You we live, move and have our being.

You are the Alpha and the Omega, the first and the last. The beginning and the end.

You preserve our lives and keep our feet from slipping.

You guard us and watch over us.

You command your angels to protect us.

Truly my soul finds rest in God; my salvation comes from Him.

You are my rock and my salvation;

You are our fortress and security, I will never be shaken.

You command the wind and the waves.

You hush the storm to silence.

Lord you are the Balm of Gilead. My healer.

You are our strength, and our champion. We can do all things through You Lord Jesus.

You are the way to the Father, we come boldly to the throne of grace because You bore our sins.

You bore our sins and carried our diseases. By Your stripes we are healed.

We are free from sin because of the price You paid.

You took our shame and the penalty due us. I am forgiven, Jesus did not die in vain.

We walk in confidence and victory because

You are the Font of all holiness.

You are the living water. Rivers of living water flow out of me because the Holy Spirit lives in me.

The same Spirit that raised Jesus from the dead lives in me.

Jesus You came to destroy the works of the devil.

You are my deliverer. You delivers me from every evil.

You are the vine, we are the branches, without You we can do nothing.

Jesus, You are the Bread of Life, my sustenance.

You are my safety, my refuge, my God in whom I trust.

You deliver me from all my fears and saves me from all my troubles.

Though the earth be shaken and the mountains quake, though the waters rage and foam and the mountains fall, I do not fear. The Lord of Hosts is with me.

Praise be to God, who has not rejected my prayer or withheld His love from me.

Lord I trust you completely because you are trustworthy. You are my Lord, my God and my King.

LITANY OF PRAISE

Praise You, Jesus, You are my life, my love.

Praise You, Jesus, You are the name above all names.

Praise You, Jesus, You are Emmanuel, God with us.

Praise You, Jesus, You are the King of Kings.

Praise You, Jesus, You are the King of creation.

Praise You, Jesus, You are King of the universe.

Praise You, Jesus, You are the Lord of lords.

Praise You, Jesus, You are the Almighty.

Praise You, Jesus, You are the Christ. Christ the King.

Praise You, Jesus, You are the Lamb of God.

Praise You, Jesus, You are Lion of Judah.

Praise You, Jesus, You are the Bright Morning Star.

Praise You, Jesus, You are our Champion and shield.

Praise You, Jesus, You are our Strength and our Song.

Praise You, Jesus, You are the way of our life.

Praise You, Jesus, You are the only truth.

Praise You, Jesus, You are the real life.

Praise You, Jesus, You are the Wonderful Counselor.

Praise You, Jesus, You are the Prince of Peace.

Praise You, Jesus, You are the Light of the World.

Praise You, Jesus, You are the Living Word.

Praise You, Jesus, You are the Redeemer.

Praise You, Jesus, You are the Anointed One.

Praise You, Jesus, You are the Holy one of Israel.

Praise You, Jesus, You are the Good Sheperd.

Praise You, Jesus, You are the Sheepgate.

Praise You, Jesus, You are the Lord of hosts.

Praise You, Jesus, You are the Rock of all ages.

Praise You, Jesus, You are my hiding place.

Praise You, Jesus, You are the Savior of the world.

Praise You, Jesus, You are the strong tower.

Praise You, Jesus, You are the Mountain Refuge.

Praise You, Jesus, You are the Bread of Life.

Praise You, Jesus, You are the Font of all holiness.

Praise You, Jesus, You are the Living Water.
Praise You, Jesus, You are the True Vine.
Praise You, Jesus, You are my Spouse. my Maker.
Praise You, Jesus, You are our Fortress.
Praise You, Jesus, You are the Deliverer.
Praise You, Jesus, You are our Victory.
Praise You, Jesus, You are our Salvation.
Praise You, Jesus, You are our Righteousness.
Praise You, Jesus, You are our Wisdom.
Praise You, Jesus, You are our Sanctification.
Praise You, Jesus, You are our Justification.
Praise You, Jesus, You are the Door.
Praise You, Jesus, You are the great I AM.
Praise You, Jesus, You are the great High Priest.
Praise You, Jesus, You are the Cornerstone.
Praise You, Jesus, You are the Sure Foundation.
Praise You, Jesus, You are our Joy. Our Portion and Cup.
Praise You, Jesus, You are my Healing and Wholeness.
Praise You, Jesus, You are our Covenant.
Praise You, Jesus, You are the Promise of the Father.
Praise You, Jesus, You are the Everlasting One.
Praise You, Jesus, You are the Most High God.
Praise You, Jesus, You are the Lamb that was slain.
Praise You, Jesus, You are the Just Judge.
Praise You, Jesus, You are the Balm of Gilead.
Praise You, Jesus, You are the Mighty Warrior.
Praise You, Jesus, You are my Defense.
Praise You, Jesus, You are the Bridegroom.
Praise You, Jesus, You are my Patience.
Praise You, Jesus, You are the Solid Reality
Praise You, Jesus, You are my Provider.
Praise You, Jesus, You are the Resurrection and the Life.
Praise You, Jesus, You are the Alpha and the Omega.
Praise You, Jesus, You are the Beginning and the End.
Praise You, Jesus, You are all that I need. You are all that I want.
You are worthy of all praise.   Amen

Pray like there is a God,
who hears and moves on your behalf.

Pray like you believe in a God that cares.

Pray with faith that can move mountains. Pray with faith that the four stretcher bearers had as they brought a man to Jesus through the roof. Pray with the faith of David before Goliath. He said "you are going down" to Goliath, a man bigger stronger and well armed. Pray with the faith of the Centurion who said "Lord just say the word and it will done." Not maybe, it will be done. Faith is believing that God WILL! Faith is not believing that God can; most everyone believes God can. It doesn't take faith to believe God can. It does, however, require faith to believe God will. Increase our faith Lord. We want to believe like you want us to believe. We want to believe like the woman whose bleeding wouldn't stop. She said. "If I just touch His cloak I will get well. Not I might get well. I will.

Mark 11: 22-25
"Have faith in God," Jesus answered.
"Truly I tell you, if anyone says to this mountain,
'Go, throw yourself into the sea,'
and does not doubt in their heart but
believes that what they say will happen,
it will be done for them. Therefore, I tell you,
whatever you ask for in prayer,
believe that you have received it, and it will be yours.
And when you stand praying,
if you hold anything against anyone, forgive them,
so that your Father in heaven
may forgive you your sins."

Made in the USA
Monee, IL
09 April 2023

31580347R10026